Teacher's
MANUAL

to

The Call of the Wild

By Nancy Romero

Talent Development Secondary Publications
Center for Social Organization of Schools
Johns Hopkins University
Baltimore

Table of Contents

TALENT DEVELOPMENT SECONDARY (TDS)

ENGLISH LANGUAGE ARTS DIVISION

MISSION STATEMENT

RESPONDING TO THE CHANGING NATURE OF LITERACY BY PROVIDING STUDENTS WITH SKILLS THAT WILL ENDURE BEYOND THE CLASSROOM

Student Team Literature Discussion Guides are designed to support teachers with organizing literacy instruction to respond to the needs of diverse student populations while striving to meet the growing instructional demands of state and district college- and career-readiness standards.

Using whole-class structures, peer discussion, and teacher modeling, this instructional framework affords students regular opportunities to engage in oral language, critical analysis and exploration of information extending to real world applications. Students intuitively deepen understanding of content and develop their inferring and evidence-gathering skills through ongoing exposure to inductive learning, a powerful strategy underlying higher-order thinking and 21st century skills. Teachers routinely facilitate small-group and whole-class discussions to help students apply academic language and develop new insights and perspectives as they read various types of authentic texts. Teachers are also encouraged and equipped to use a variety of informational texts in conjunction with literary works, and to provide students with the skills they need to comprehend these increasingly complex texts. Through reading and writing for different purposes and from multiple perspectives, students move toward the self-regulated learning and independent thinking required to function in today's society.

In the midst of the flow of information surrounding adolescent literacy, we recognize the significant role that motivation plays in the lives of adolescent learners. The instructional design and materials used in the TDS program enable students to exercise mental processes needed to comprehend, communicate, reason, evaluate, and persevere. Students take ownership of learning experiences and make choices within a responsive, student-centered classroom environment.

With the growing demands of the 21st century, the TDS ELA Discussion Guides offer flexibility and guidance to teachers who seek specific focus and clarity when planning instruction. Teachers are able to build instructional modules around core reading selections using existing approaches and activities contained in the Discussion Guides. This approach helps establish historical and factual connections, and addresses specific assessments, standards and skills in the context of teaching the core reading selections. Using this method to planning and teaching literacy, classroom teachers and TDS instructional support staff can effectively collaborate around core approaches to promote achievement for all students in the 21st century.

To the Teacher

This Teacher's Manual is part of a research-based, cooperative approach to teaching literature developed by the Talent Development Secondary Program at the Johns Hopkins University. This approach, called Student Team Literature, strengthens students' thinking, reading, writing, and social skills. In Student Team Literature, students read quality books and work in learning teams using *Student Discussion Guides* that lead them to become critical thinkers, expand their working vocabularies, and broaden their knowledge of the writer's craft. Guides are available to support study of over 70 novels, biographies, and short story and poetry collections. Students read the literature and work through a Student Discussion Guide using a weekly cycle of instruction.

Each Student Discussion Guide includes the following components:

- **Vocabulary Lists** expose students to terms they need to know in order to understand what they are reading.

- **Starred High Frequency Words** are those that students acquire for their working vocabularies, as they occur often in many contexts. Students learn to use these words in meaningful sentences that include context clues to show understanding of the new words.

- **Writer's Craft Boxes** provide information about aspects of the writer's craft (e.g., flashbacks, figurative language) that students encounter in the literature. Craft Boxes can be used as the basis for mini-lessons.

- **Questions** and **Graphic Organizers** lead students to analyze the literature, organize information, and better understand the writer's message.

- **Make a Prediction** and **What If? Boxes** lead students to establish expectations about what will come next in their reading.

- **Selection Review** questions and answers are used by pairs of students to prepare for literature tests.

- **Literature-related Writing** suggestions lead students to respond to literature and try various forms of writing.

- **Extension Activities** give students opportunities to express themselves in response to the text through art, drama, research, and other activities.

- **So, You Want to Read More...** suggests books for independent reading that match the one students have read in theme, genre, or topic.

- **About the Author** provides biographical information, as well as listing some of the writer's other works.

In addition to these sections, each Teacher's Manual also includes:

- a **Summary** of the book or literary work

- a **Building Background** section with suggestions for preparing students to read the literary work

- a **Preview/Predict/Purpose** section with questions that lead students to establish expectations before beginning to read

- **Guided Discussion** questions and suggestions for whole-class discussions

- **Listening Comprehension/Read Aloud Connections** identifying relevant literary elements and devices and listing short works that include these features, which teachers can use to prepare and present *Listening Comprehension* lessons (a teacher read-aloud/think-aloud activity that serves as a companion to Student Team Literature)

These materials can be used within or outside the context of the Student Team Literature program, although we believe teachers who have been trained in the program make the best use of them. (Please see below for teacher training contact information.)

About the Literature

The most effective motivation for adolescent readers lies in the relevance of the literature they are presented. Poor or reluctant readers are particularly in need of relevance in the written word. They need to see themselves in the pages they turn.

Today's adolescents are fortunate; never have they had so much quality literature available that reflects their experiences, their problems, and their cultures. The driving force behind Student Team Literature is making accessible the best of middle grades literature. Discussion Guides have been written for a wide variety of literary works at every readability level, from high interest/low readability selections to classic literature used in middle grades English language arts instruction for over twenty-five years.

The Weekly Instruction Cycle

Discussion Guides enable teachers to lead learning teams through literary works in a cycle of activities that includes **direct instruction**, **team practice and discussion**, and **individual assessment**. After careful preliminary vocabulary instruction, students: (1) read a selected text portion silently; (2) complete (optional) Partner Reading, which gives poor readers and second language learners additional practice to build fluency by reading excerpts aloud; (3) discuss with their partners possible responses to questions and activities in Student Discussion Guides; and, (4) write individual responses to the questions and activities.

Discussion Guides and Cooperative Learning

Discussion Guides are designed to be used in the classroom in the context of cooperative learning. Cooperative learning requires students to learn and exercise many social and academic skills, beginning with the most basic, such as active listening and staying on task. For that reason, introducing students (and teachers, during professional development) to Student Team Literature typically involves direct instruction in relevant skills. The teacher determines the skills to be taught (one at a time), the order in which they will be introduced, and students' readiness to add new skills. Instruction includes discussion of the skill and its importance; completion of a T-chart to show what the skill looks and sounds like (making abstract social skills more concrete for students); and modeling and role-playing use of the skill. As students apply the skills in daily classroom activities, teachers monitor and reinforce their use. Students gradually internalize the skills, creating a cooperative learning climate that has an important positive impact on classroom management and academic achievement.

Assessment

Three assessment tools are available to teachers who use Student Team Literature guides. Each week, after quizzing each other in a process called "Selection Review," students take **literature tests** that require short constructed responses. **Vocabulary tests** assess students' ability to compose meaningful sentences using the high frequency words they have studied in the context of the literature. These Selection Reviews, literature tests, and vocabulary tests are provided on reproducible pages at the end of each Teacher's Manual. In addition, students can practice their standardized test taking skills in relation to the literary work they have studied by taking Standardized Reading Practice Tests that are similar in format to the standardized tests used in school districts throughout the country. Standardized Reading Practice Tests must be ordered separately.

Ordering information

The Talent Development Secondary program offers Teacher's Manuals, Student Discussion Guides, and a Standardized Reading Practice Test booklet including reproducible assessment pages.

- To place an order, call 410-516-4339 or email tds@jhu.edu. The complete Talent Development Secondary materials catalog is available online on our website (see below).

- For teacher training or more on our English language arts, math, science, or social studies programs, contact Maria Waltemeyer at 410-516-2247 or mwaltemeyer@jhu.edu

- Also visit our website at
  www.talentdevelopmentsecondary.com/curriculum

About The Author

Jack London was born in 1875 in a poverty-stricken area in Oakland, California. London was born out of wedlock and never knew his true father. London had a difficult childhood, and by age 15 he was a sailor bound for Japan and the Siberian coast. When he returned to the United States, he lived as a vagrant until he decided to enroll in college to further his education. As a student at the University of California, London became interested in politics and writing. He was concerned about the mistreatment of poor, working people. He was also interested in socialism and Charles Darwin's theory of evolution.

Jack London was a traveler, and his journeys took him to the Alaskan wilderness at the time of the Alaskan gold rush.

continued on page 2

The Call of the Wild

By Jack London

Teacher's Manual
Suggested length of time to be spent on this novel: 4 weeks

Summary

Jack London's *The Call of the Wild* is the story of a dog named Buck who is stolen from his affluent, sheltered life in California and sold as a sled dog in the harsh Alaskan wilderness. Buck is able to adapt to this radical change, however, and adapts better and more quickly than other dogs who have been sold to work in the North. Buck learns quickly that the laws that governed his life in the civilized Santa Clara Valley do not apply in the uncivilized Northland. The North is ruled by the law of the club (human force) and the law of the fang (animal violence). Buck's ability to conquer both these laws makes him a survivor and a leader in the Northland.

Through a succession of masters and journeys, Buck struggles to survive. His experiences take him farther and farther away from his civilized self. It is Buck's reliance on his animal instincts and his gradual return to a more primitive state that enable him to rise above both the animals and humans in the story. It is also clear that Buck's inherited characteristics, his huge, strong body and natural cunning, are significant factors in his survival.

Buck's story is complete when he severs all connections to civilization and obeys the call of the wild that has beckoned him throughout the story. He learns to conquer both animal and man. His incredible achievements make him a legend among the Yeehat Indians, and in mating with wild timber wolves, he creates a new breed.

About
The Author

(cont.)

**This experience pro-
vided the setting for
many of London's
novels, including his
most famous, *The
Call of the Wild*. This
novel, published in
1902, was one of
London's first and
brought him instant
acclaim and fame.
He became one of
the most popular and
successful writers of
his day. London was
plagued by numerous
health problems,
however. He became
dependent on the
drugs that he took
for his pain. He died
from an overdose of
drugs at the age of
forty, an overdose
that many believe
was intentional.**

Building Background

A brief background on the setting of this novel is helpful to the reader, though it is alluded to in the first chapter. Gold was found in the late 1800's in the Klondike region of Canada near the Alaskan border. Men quit their jobs and left their homes and families to travel to the Klondike in hope of "striking it rich." Dog sleds were used to pull loads across the frozen Alaskan wilderness on the way to the Klondike region. Prepare to introduce the novel by securing maps that students can use to locate California and Canada's Klondike region. They can trace the route Buck travels as they read the novel.

An understanding of Jack London's personal philosophy is also essential to the reading of *The Call of the Wild*. London was considered a writer of naturalism. Naturalism is the belief that man is controlled by his environment. In his novels, people and animals contend with the social, economic, and physical elements in their surroundings.

London was also fascinated with Charles Darwin's theory of evolution and his concept of the "survival of the fittest." Who survives in a particular environment is determined by who is strongest and most adaptable to the surroundings. This "survival of the fittest" theme, or the "law of the club and the fang," as it is referred to in *The Call of the Wild*, is the novel's strongest theme. Evolution is also a major premise of the novel.

The Call of the Wild did not necessarily gain its popularity from London's philosophy of life, however. Many love the story for its sense of adventure. It is an escape from a routine, civilized life to an exciting, perilous, uncivilized one. It appeals to every person's longing to leave behind the entanglements of everyday life to commune with nature.

It is also important to note that *The Call of the Wild* is episodic. Each chapter is a story in itself with its own climax and conclusion. Buck, a dog who survives the harsh wilderness because he returns to a more primitive state, is the main character in every chapter.

So, You
Want To Read
More

If you enjoyed *The Call of the Wild*, you may want to read its companion novel, *White Fang*. Also written by Jack London, *White Fang* tells the story of a wild Northland dog that becomes civilized.

Other wilderness adventure stories are Gary Paulsen's *Hatchet*, Armstrong Sperry's *Call It Courage*, Theodore Taylor's *The Cay*, and Scott O'Dell's *The Island of the Blue Dolphins*. The Adventures of Huckleberry Finn by Mark Twain and *Treasure Island* by Robert Louis Stevenson are classic adventure stories.

Listening Comprehension/Read Aloud Connections

The Call of the Wild is an **adventure story**. The novel's main character, Buck, has sometimes been compared to the character Huck in Mark Twain's Huckleberry Finn. You may read a portion of Huckleberry Finn to emphasize its portrayal of adventure and its **characterization** of Huck Finn.

The **setting** is of utmost importance in *The Call of the Wild*. Though almost any piece of young children's literature can be used to help students understand the concept of setting, the first page of *Black Cowboy/Wild Horses: A True Story* by Julius Lester and Jerry Pinkney provides a particularly wonderful example of setting, as does the first line of *Mufaro's Beautiful Daughters: An African Tale* by John Steptoe. In addition, mysteries written at almost any readability level often contain examples of finely drawn settings.

Although the animals in *The Call of the Wild* do not speak or perform feats beyond the abilities of real dogs, many of the animals' thoughts, feelings, and motivations are human. Such characters are **anthropomorphic**. Examples of similar kinds of animal stories are fables. You may want to read selections from *Aesop's Fables* or Shirley Climo's *King of the Birds.*

Symbolism and **foreshadowing** are used often in this novel. *Jumanji* by Chris Van Allsburg contains foreshadowing. Symbolism is used in Van Allsburg's *The Wretched Stone*. You may also read a Robert Frost poem, such as "Mending Wall," "Stopping by the Woods on a Snowy Evening," or "The Road Not Taken," to focus on symbolism.

Preview/Predict/Purpose

To **preview** the novel, have students examine its front and back covers, noting any illustrations and text. Have them note the title of the book and the title of the first chapter. Read the poem at the beginning of the first chapter and discuss it. It will be necessary to define several words such as *nomadic* (having a wandering way of life with no permanent home), *chafing* (wearing away by rubbing), *brumal* (wintry), and *ferine* (wild or savage). This poem introduces a major theme in *The Call of the Wild*. It speaks of primitive qualities awakening after a long sleep.

Give a brief background on the Klondike region gold rush, also referred to as the Alaskan gold rush. Buck, the main character in *The Call of the Wild*, is a dog that pulls one of the sleds used to carry loads to and from the Klondike. Lead the students to find California, Alaska, and Canada's Klondike region on maps.

Ask students to guess what it means for Buck, who is an animal, to awaken to a more primitive, animalistic state. Ask students to speculate concerning the meaning of the story's title.

Invite students to read the remaining chapter titles and to note any illustrations in the book. Have students **predict** the kind of adventures and challenges Buck will have.

Have students use their predictions to set a **purpose** for reading. Students might want to discover the meaning of the story's title. Students might want to learn how an animal can become more primitive. Students might want to discover the story's themes.

Discussion Guide #1

Chapters 1 and 2

Write the starred words on the **VOCABULARY LIST** on page 7 and their definitions on chart paper or sentence strips that will remain posted throughout the time that students work on the Discussion Guide.

Prepare a Vocabulary Prediction Chart (see illustration below) for students to complete after you have introduced the reading selection and the **VOCABULARY LIST**, and before they have begun to read. The chart contains categories into which starred words from the list are to be placed. Students predict how each starred word relates to the reading selection, or if it is impossible to predict its relationship. Categories can be adjusted according to the type of literature being read.

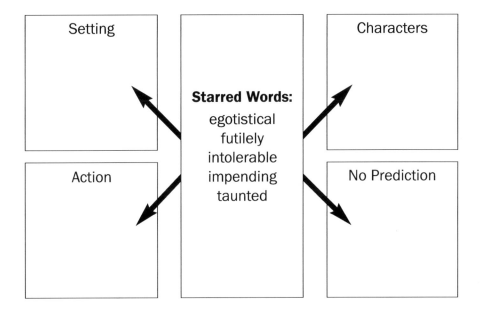

First, read aloud the list of words in the order in which they appear. Second, reread the words and have students repeat each one after you. Third, ask students if they know the definitions of any of the words. Confirm correct definitions, or, in the case of multiple meaning words, identify definitions that match the context in which the words are used in the story. Next, ask students if they recognize parts of unfamiliar words. If students' decoding skills are below level, stress at this time the sounds of syllables — especially in starred words. In all cases, use this time to focus on identifying the meanings of any prefixes, suffixes or roots that are contained in unfamiliar words, and lead students to formulate definitions based upon the meanings of their parts. Finally, provide definitions for any words that remain undefined. **(Definitions of starred words are in the glossaries that follow the Vocabulary Lists. Definitions are *not* provided for the other words in the Vocabulary Lists.)**

Reread the list in random order and have students repeat each word after you. Then point to the words in random order and have the students pronounce each one without your assistance. Return to any words that students have difficulty pronouncing until they can pronounce them correctly. **This process will be repeated each day that students are working on a particular Discussion Guide, so if students still have difficulty pronouncing some of the words, they will have other opportunities for practice and correction.**

Next, lead students in completing the Vocabulary Prediction Chart. The importance of this activity lies in encouraging students to make logical connections between what they have been told about the reading selection and specific vocabulary words. **Being correct about predictions is not important; the thought process required to make predictions is.** The graphic organizer should be put on chart paper so that the list can remain posted as students read the section of the reading selection in which the words first appear. Introduce words in subsequent Discussion Guides similarly.

Vocabulary List A

paddocks (p.3)
imperiously (p. 3)
sated (p. 3)
aristocrat (p. 3)
trifle (adv., p. 3)
*egotistical (p. 3)
insular (p. 3)
pampered (adj., p. 3)
progeny (p. 4)
rage (n., p. 5)

deft (p. 5)
*futilely (p. 5)
vilely (p. 5)
ebbed (p. 5)
*intolerable (p. 6)
*impending (p. 7)
calamity (p. 7)
unkempt p. 7)
*taunted (v., p. 8)
waxed (p. 8)

parched (adj., p. 8)
metamorphosed (p. 9)
fiend (p. 9)
gingerly (p. 9)
uncowed (p. 12)
conciliated (p. 13)
uncouth (p. 13)
wheedlingly (p. 13)
swarthy (p. 14)

Special Glossary

artesian well - a kind of well built so that groundwater flows upwards out of a well without the need for pumping.

demesne - a large piece of land owned by one person; an estate

pent - penned; held or kept in

Santa Clara Valley - an area in Western California near the city of San Jose

Puget Sound - an inlet off the ocean that lies off the coast of the state of Washington

Arctic - the region around the North Pole

Northland - a term used by Jack London to refer to the cold, harsh region north of the continental United States

Klondike strike - reference to the gold rush that occurred in the 1800s in the Klondike region of Canada near the Alaskan border

hydrophoby - a disease potentially fatal to humans that is spread by bites from infected animals, also known as rabies

sacredam - a mild French Canadian curse word

Southland - a term used by Jack London to refer to Buck's home-land, the region south of the Alaskan and Canadian borders

dispatches - official messages or mail

Geological Survey - government organization that studies the environment

continued...

the Barrens - a vast, frozen area in northern Canada where few plants grow

Queen Charlotte Sound - a deep, wide inlet off the Pacific Ocean that lies off the coast of western Canada

Glossary of Starred Words

egotistical - self-centered

futilely - hopelessly

intolerable - unbearable; hard to deal with

impending - about to happen; upcoming

taunted - teased; ridiculed; mocked

Sample Meaningful Sentences for Starred Words

1. Damon was **egotistical** and only enjoyed talking about himself.

2. Kara groaned **futilely** as the runner passed her because she knew there was no chance she could catch up and win the race.

3. Elaine found the hot Florida climate **intolerable**, so she moved back to New England where the summers were much cooler.

4. Jake was sure there must be an **impending** quiz in Spanish class because they had not had a quiz for several weeks.

5. Because Philip's classmates **taunted** him about the clothes he wore, he felt ashamed of the way he looked.

The Writer's Craft

Characterization

Characterization is the way an author develops characters so that readers can picture them and understand their feelings and actions. An author can give readers descriptions of characters, or use characters' words, actions, or thoughts to help them learn what the characters are like. The characterization in *The Call of the Wild* is unusual because the main character, Buck, is a dog. Think about Jack London's characterization of Buck as you read the first chapter of the novel. Consider the kinds of words or phrases you would use to describe Buck's character. Do you think Buck acts and thinks more like a dog or like a human?

DISCUSSION QUESTIONS AND ACTIVITIES

Section I. Read chapter 1 (pages 1-16). Discuss your responses to the questions and activities with a classmate. Then write your answers independently.

1. **Why is Buck sold? Why are Buck and other dogs like him in demand along the Pacific Coast?** A man working for Buck's owner needs money, so he sells Buck without the owner's knowledge. Gold has been found in the Arctic, and many men are rushing there in hopes of finding gold. The men need strong, long-haired dogs to pull their sleds through the frozen wilderness.

2. **Why is Buck shocked by the treatment he receives after he is sold? What unforgettable lesson does "the club" teach him?** Buck has had a pleasant, easy life in the Santa Clara Valley. He has never been treated cruelly or beaten. This is why he is shocked when he is beaten and treated harshly after being sold. The club, which Buck has never faced before, introduces him to the "reign of primitive law." The encounter

makes Buck wiser, because he knows he cannot beat a man with a club. Life has taken on a fiercer aspect than Buck had ever known in his gentle, carefree days in "the sun-kissed Santa Clara Valley."

3. **Describe both Buck's human- and dog-like qualities.** Buck is entirely dog-like in his behavior. He makes dog-like sounds and performs dog-like behaviors. Buck's thoughts, desires, and ambitions, however, are described in human-like terms. For example, Buck is described as egotistical and prideful in his home in Santa Clara. Though it is possible for a dog to be self-centered, London's description of Buck's character goes beyond what one would normally expect of a dog. Buck is described as purposefully preventing himself from becoming a "mere pampered house-dog" by taking part in challenging out-door activities. Buck's thought process as he learns from his harsh treatment and the treatment of the other dogs is also very human-like.

4. **Who are Francois and Perrault, and why does Buck respect them?** Francois and Perrault are French-Canadians who work as dispatchers for the Canadian government. They have purchased Buck and several other dogs to help in their work. Buck respects them because they are fair, calm, and wise in the way of dogs.

5. **What shows that Buck is already beginning to adapt to his new surroundings?** When Buck is first exposed to his new harsh lifestyle, he becomes filled with uncontrollable anger and uses all of his energy to lash out at anyone nearby. When he learns that he doesn't stand a chance "against a man with a club," he becomes a more obedient dog. Though the text states that Buck has not been broken, he has become smarter in his dealings with men. Buck is learning to do what he must do to survive in his new situation.

Make A
Prediction:

**How will Buck cope
in his new life in the
harsh Arctic?**

**How will all of the
dogs owned by
Francois and Perrault
interact with one
another?**

**What other lessons
will Buck learn?**

Guided Discussion:

Discuss some of the key questions and activities in Section I of the Discussion Guide. In addition, feel free to include in your discussion questions that are not in the Discussion Guide, such as: *In what ways are the men described in this chapter similar to animals? How is Buck's new lifestyle different from his old one?*

Vocabulary Prediction Check-up

Return to the vocabulary prediction chart, and use it to check the predictions students made prior to reading this section of the reading selection. Remind students that, even if their predictions did not prove true, the value was in making them.

Vocabulary List B

imperative (adj., p. 17)	belligerent (p. 20)	animated (p. 24)
vicarious (p. 17)	ignominiously (p. 21)	retaliate (p. 25)
draught (p. 19)	forlorn (p. 22)	routed (p. 26)
*perpetual (p. 20)	spasmodically (p. 23)	fastidiousness (p. 27)
*malignant (p. 20)	arduous (p. 23)	*callous (adj., p. 28)
incarnation (p. 20)	placatingly (p. 23)	*conspicuous (p. 29)
prowess (p. 20)	*despise (p. 24)	leeward (p. 29)

Special Glossary

primordial - primitive; that which has existed from the beginning

civilization - social organization of a higher order, marked by such things as the development of a written language, the arts and sciences, government, etc.

moral nature - the ability to tell the difference between right and wrong

Glossary of Starred Words

perpetual - never ending

malignant - evil; dangerous

despise - to strongly dislike

callous - hardened; insensitive; indifferent

conspicuous - well-defined; observable; easy to see

Sample Meaningful Sentences for Starred Words

1. "Living on that planet would be like living in a **perpetual** storm," explained the science teacher, "because strong winds are always swirling around it."

2. There was something **malignant** about the strangeness in the sky and the air, so Gabriela became frightened and hurried home.

3. Because Denise's weekly visits to the doctor were painful, she began to **despise** them and begged her mother to stop taking her.

4. Mark used to cry whenever his father left home, but he eventually became **callous** to his father's many absences, and the situation no longer seemed to affect him.

5. "My house is so **conspicuous** sitting alone of the top of a hill that you can't miss it," explained Darryl as he gave directions.

The Writer's Craft

Contrast

Contrast occurs when an opposing idea or thing is presented for the sake of emphasis or clearness. Jack London uses contrast often in the beginning of *The Call of the Wild.* In the first chapter, London contrasts Buck's earlier lifestyle in the Southland with his new lifestyle in the Northland. As you read chapter 2, notice how London further develops this contrast. Why do you think he does this?

DISCUSSION QUESTIONS AND ACTIVITIES

Section II. Read chapter 2 (pages 17-30). Discuss answers to the following questions with a classmate, then write your answers independently.

1. **What does Buck learn from Curly's death? How does Curly's death change Buck's relationship with Spitz?** When Curly is viciously attacked and killed by another dog, Buck knows that there is no fair play in the land of the North. He begins to hate Spitz bitterly because he laughs at the attack on Curly.

2. **What is "the law of the club and the fang," the law followed by both dogs and men in the Northland? What incidents have taught this law to Buck?** The law of the club and the fang is the rule of power and brute force. Buck learns the law of the club from the red-sweatered man in chapter 1, who brutally beats him into submission. Buck learns the law of the fang from the vicious attack on Curly.

3. **Contrast life in the Southland with life in the Northland. How has Buck changed to adapt to his new life in the Northland?** The Southland is a civilized, gentle society ruled by the law of love and fellowship. Private property and personal feelings are respected in the Southland. In contrast, the

Northland is a savage, hostile environment ruled by the law of club and the fang. Buck has rejected the morality of the Southland which is "a handicap in the ruthless struggle for existence." He has learned to steal when he is hungry. Physically, he has also adapted. He has grown callous to ordinary pain, learned to eat whatever is available, and heightened his senses.

4. **London compares the contrast between the Southland and the Northland with the contrast between civilization and "things primordial." What is London trying to communicate through this comparison?** London is stating that the moral, pleasant life in the Southland is a product of civilization. The "ruthless struggle" that is characteristic of life in the Northland is primitive; in other words, it reflects more closely the original nature of both man and animal. Buck is beginning to live by his instincts, his uncivilized self, in order to survive.

5. **Why has Buck's adaptation to the hostile environment of the Northland been easy and rapid?** Buck has adapted well because he is a quick learner, but also because the instincts of his ancestors have come alive in him. Though he has been a domesticated animal, he has begun to sense a kinship with his wild ancestors, and the instincts and qualities that they possessed for survival are becoming his own.

Make A Prediction:

What new problems will Buck encounter as he continues to travel through the Northland?

Guided Discussion:

Discuss some of the key questions and activities in Section II. In addition, feel free to include in your discussion questions that are not in the Discussion Guide, such as:

- *What are the dogs in Buck's team like? Describe each of their personalities.*

- *What does author Jack London mean when he states that Buck's moral nature was a handicap in his struggle for existence? Do you agree or disagree with this idea?*

- *Describe the contrast between the team's two newest dogs, Billie and Joe. Which is more likely to survive? Why?*

Vocabulary Prediction Check-up

Return to the vocabulary prediction chart, and use it to check the predictions students made prior to reading this section of the reading selection. Remind students that, even if their predictions did not prove true, the value was in making them.

 Selection Review

1. **Why does Buck come to the Northland? Why are Buck's new circumstances so shocking to him?** A man working for Buck's owner needs money, so he sells Buck without the owner's knowledge. Buck is sold to men in the Northland, the cold harsh region north of the continental United States. There is a gold rush in the Northland. The men who search for gold need strong, long-haired dogs to pull their sleds through the frozen wilderness. Buck has been used to a pleasant, easy life in the Santa Clara Valley. After he is sold he is shocked by the harsh, cruel treatment he receives.

2. **Explain the statement, "[Buck] had been suddenly jerked from the heart of civilization and flung into the heart of things primordial." Use examples from the novel to support your answer.** Author Jack London associates the pleasant, orderly, moral lifestyle of the Southland with civilization. He associates the harsh struggle and the unfair, immoral nature of the Northland with primitive life. This statement means that Buck has been taken away from a civilized life and placed in a primitive one.

3. **What is the "law of the club and fang," and how does Buck learn it?** The law of the club and the fang is the rule of power and physical force. Buck learns the law of the club from the red-sweatered man in chapter 1, who beats Buck into obedience. Buck learns the law of the fang from the terrible attack on Curly.

4. **How does Buck begin to change in order to survive in his new surroundings?** In order to survive, Buck has to forget the way he interacted with other animals and people in the Southland. Buck begins to depend on his instincts to survive. He rejects the morality of the Southland, which is "a handicap in the ruthless struggle for existence." He learns to steal when he is hungry. Physically, he also adapts. He becomes hardened toward ordinary pain, learns to eat whatever is available, and develops sharper senses.

5. **Describe Buck's relationship with Spitz, the leader of the dog team. Make a prediction about their relationship, giving reasons to support your prediction.** Spitz, the dog team leader, is described as a smart, skilled sled team leader. However, he has a hardened, cruel nature, which angers Buck. Spitz laughs when Curly is killed by a group of other dogs. When Buck sees this, he begins to hate Spitz "with a bitter and deathless hatred." This description of Buck's feelings towards Spitz is so strong, it hints at a future conflict between the two dogs. Predictions about the nature of this conflict will vary. Be sure you present reasons that support your predictions.

 Literature-Related Writing

1. If Buck could write a **letter** to his former owner, Judge Miller, about his new life in the Northland, what would he write? Would he express a desire to return to the Southland or not? Write a letter from Buck to Judge Miller expressing his thoughts.

2. Write a **poem** that describes the "law of the club and the fang."

3. Pretend you are an animal rights activist living during the time of the Klondike gold rush. Write an **editorial** about the treatment of sled dogs used by the men searching for gold.

Extension Activities

1. Draw two contrasting pictures—one depicting life for Buck in the Santa Clara Valley and another depicting life in the frozen Northland.

2. Research the Klondike-region gold rush of the late 1800s. Share what you learn with your classmates.

Literature Test

1. **What law rules the Northland? Describe this law.** The law of the club and the fang rules the Northland. It is a rule by power and brute force.

2. **How is life in the Southland different from life in the Northland?** The Southland is a civilized, gentle society ruled by the law of love and fellowship. Private property and personal feelings are respected in the Southland. In contrast, the Northland is a savage, hostile environment ruled by the law of club and the fang.

3. **What changes in Buck show that he is "fit to survive" in the Northland?** In order to survive, Buck has to forget the way he interacted with other animals and people in the Southland. Buck begins to rely on his instincts to survive. He rejects the morality of the Southland, which is "a handicap in the ruthless struggle for existence." He learns to steal when he is hungry. Physically, he also adapts. He becomes hardened toward ordinary pain, learns to eat whatever is available, and develops sharper senses.

4. **What does author Jack London mean when he describes the Northland as being "primordial"?** London is stating that the "ruthless struggle" that is characteristic of life in the Northland is primitive; in other words, it reflects more closely the original nature of both man and animal. Buck is beginning to live by his instincts, his uncivilized self, in order to survive.

5. **How do you think Buck's view of men and animals has changed as a result of his experiences in the Northland? Explain your answer.** Students' answers will vary. Accept supported responses. Students should note that Buck has a much lower view of both men and animals as a result of his experiences. Buck, who never questioned the actions or motives of the man who sold him to the Northland, will be much less trusting of men in the future. He now knows that both men and animals can be cruel and unfair. He is also more likely to be cruel and unfair himself. The law of the club and the fang rules in the north, and Buck must abide by it in order to survive.

Discussion Guide #2

Chapters 3 and 4

Vocabulary List A

*dominant (p. 31)	jugular (n., p. 34)	insubordination (p. 42)
cunning (n., p. 31)	*daunted (p. 36)	
poise (n., p. 31)	dubiously (p. 36)	insidious (p. 44)
pandemonium (p. 33)	*defied (p. 36)	*rampant (p. 47)
skulking (p. 33)	*shirked (p. 41)	exultantly (p. 49)
malingerer (p. 34)	prostrate (adj., p. 41)	inexorable (p. 50)
adversary (p. 34)	abjectly (p. 41)	
din (p. 34)	covert (p. 42)	

Special Glossary

score - twenty people or things

eddies - small whirlpools

aurora borealis - streamer-like colored lights seen in the sky near the North Pole; also known as the Northern Lights

Glossary of Starred Words

dominant - ruling; strongest

daunted - discouraged

defied - opposed; disobeyed

shirked - avoided; neglected; refused to carry out a responsibility or job

rampant - running wild; unchecked; not held back

Sample Meaningful Sentences for Starred Words

1. Julie had a **dominant** personality and was clearly the leader of the group, as she barked order after order to other group members.

2. Kerry was not **daunted** by the long, steep path that lay ahead, even though she was tired and had already traveled a great distance.

3. Mr. Parker told all of the orchestra members to wear black ties, but Charles **defied** him and wore a red one instead.

4. Though Tara was supposed to wash the dishes, she **shirked** the job and watched TV instead.

5. Rumors about the cafeteria fight were **rampant** throughout the school, and Mira heard students tell three different versions of what happened as she walked between classes.

 The Writer's Craft

Figurative Language

Jack London uses **figurative language** often in *The Call of the Wild*. Figurative language is language used to describe by means of comparisons. A **simile** is a comparison introduced by "like" or "as," for example, "Joe was snapping like a demon" (p. 34). In this simile, Joe's behavior is compared to that of a demon. Like the simile, the **metaphor** compares two things, but it does not contain the words "like" or "as." It states or implies that one thing is another. For example, "...and Toots and Ysabel [Buck] utterly ignored, for he was king... (p. 3). In this metaphor, Buck is called a king because this is how he views himself. He ignores the other dogs because he considers them less important than himself.

continued...

Personification is the giving of human attributes to an animal or an object. For example, the statement, "My hair never obeys me," is personification because the hair is described as having a human characteristic, the ability to disobey. As you read the following section, look for more examples of these types of figurative language.

DISCUSSION QUESTIONS AND ACTIVITIES

Section I. Read chapter 3 (pages 31-51). Discuss answers to the following questions with a classmate, then write your answers independently.

1. **A major theme in this novel is the fight for survival. List several incidents in chapter 3 that bring out this theme.** The starving huskies who raid the camp are driven by their hunger and viciously attack the dogs in camp in order to find food for their survival. Both the men and the dogs show incredible stamina and persistence in their trek on the hazardous trail. Whenever a man or dog slips through the ice into the water, the group must stop and build a fire to dry out. Otherwise, they will die. The ultimate fight for survival comes when Buck and Spitz fight to the death in the climax of this chapter.

2. **According to the narrator, what does Buck learn from the red-sweatered man that makes him so dangerous?** Buck learns patience from the red-sweatered man. Buck is unable to defeat the man even though he is filled with rage and does everything in his power to fight him. Buck learns that he cannot win against a man with a club. Buck learns that waging an all-out fight is not necessarily the best way to win a battle. Buck has gained cunning and has learned to fight his opponents in less obvious ways. For example, Buck begins to fight Spitz by undermining his leadership in the dog team. Because he does not fight with his muscles only, but also with his cleverness, he is unusually dangerous.

3. **How does Buck and Spitz's battle for leadership affect the dog sled team?** When Buck openly and continually challenges Spitz's leadership of the dog sled team, the team becomes much less effective in its work. The dogs quarrel among themselves and do not work together.

4. **Although Spitz is a much more experienced fighter, Buck is able to defeat him. Why is Buck able to kill Spitz?** When Spitz and Buck fight by instinct, Spitz dominates the fight. Buck changes his strategy. He uses his mind to overcome Spitz. Buck devises a clever trick to cripple and kill him.

5. **What descriptions in this chapter show that Buck has become completely primitive?** Several descriptions in this chapter show that Buck has completely returned to his primitive state and now lives as his ancestors lived. It is stated at the beginning of the chapter that the primordial beast within Buck has been growing stronger and stronger. The night that the dog sled team arrives in Dawson, Buck is drawn to the howling of the huskies. It is an "old song," a primitive song, with which Buck completely identifies. The narrator states that because Buck was stirred by the "song," it showed how completely Buck has returned to "life in the howling ages." Buck feels more alive than ever when he is pursuing the rabbit. His longing to kill is an ecstatic experience. Finally, Buck's compelling need to face Spitz and assume the leadership of the dog team also reflects his primitive self.

Make A Prediction:

Will the dog sled team respond to Spitz's death? Will the dogs continue to cause trouble for Francois and Perrault?

Guided Discussion:

Discuss some of the key questions in Section I. In addition, feel free to include in your discussion questions that are not in the Discussion Guide, such as:

* *How is Buck's longing to kill compared to man's longing? Why do you think the author makes this comparison?*

continued...

- *What kind of men are Francois and Perrault? How would you feel about taking over their jobs?*

- *What examples of figurative language did you find?*
Possible answers include:
Similes: "Driving snow, a wind that cut like a hot-white knife..." p. 31; "Twice his teeth clipped together, like the steel jaws of a trap..." p. 47.
Personification: "Its wild water defied the frost..." p. 36; "He skirted the frowning shores..." p. 36.
Metaphors: London uses several metaphors in this chapter to refer to the primitive life. The "old song" (p. 43) of the huskies is a reference to this. Buck is said to be going back into the "womb of Time" as he becomes more primitive. (p. 46). This metaphor also contains personification as time is said to have a "womb." The references to Life and Death (p. 47) during the rabbit chase are also examples of metaphors and personification.

 Vocabulary Prediction Check-up

Return to the vocabulary prediction chart, and use it to check the predictions students made prior to reading this section of the reading selection. Remind students that, even if their predictions did not prove true, the value was in making them.

Vocabulary List B

*coveted (adj., p. 52)	celerity (p. 56)	suppressedly (p. 61)
obdurate (p. 53)	*monotonous (p. 58)	lugubriously (p. 63)
forevalued (p. 54)	*potent (p. 59)	
*sheepishly (p. 54)	resiliency (p. 60)	

Special Glossary

Scotch - of or about the country of Scotland (usually "Scottish")

half-breed - a rude term for a person whose parents are of different ethnic groups

Glossary of Starred Words

coveted - longed for with envy; strongly desired

sheepishly - with embarrassment

monotonous - boring; routine; uneventful

potent - powerful

Sample Meaningful Sentences for Starred Words

1. Jorge **coveted** the trophy to be awarded to the best speaker, so he worked hard to do his best in the competition.

2. When Leo realized he was wearing two differently colored socks, he looked **sheepishly** at people around him and tucked his feet under his chair.

3. Katie felt that it was **monotonous** to run around the track, so she ran through her neighborhood where there were interesting things to see.

4. Since Edward was not feeling better, the doctor ordered a more **potent** medicine that he thought would be strong enough to take care of the problem.

DISCUSSION QUESTIONS AND ACTIVITIES

Section II. Read chapter 4 (pages 52-65). Discuss answers to the following questions with a classmate, then write your answers independently.

1. **Buck conquered "the law of the fang" in his cunning and savage defeat of Spitz. How does he conquer the "law of the club" in this chapter?** Buck refuses to harness with the team when he realizes that the men are not going to make him the lead dog. Francois gets a club to beat Buck into submission, but Buck has become wise in the way of the club. Buck keeps clear of the club and keeps running to avoid capture. After an hour of running after Buck, the men relent, put down their club, and harness Buck in as the lead dog of the sled team.

2. **What kind of leader is Buck?** Buck is an outstanding dog team leader. Buck has to retrain the unruly dogs, and he trains them well. The dogs begin to run with solidarity once again, and the team makes record time.

3. **What do you learn about Buck from his dreams?** Buck still has fond memories of his home in the Santa Clara Valley, but he is not homesick and has no desire to return to his former way of life. Much stronger are his visions of his ancestors. These overwhelming dreams of prehistoric existence reflect the change in Buck's inner state. He is no longer the civilized dog of the Southland, but is becoming more and more like his uncivilized ancestors.

4. **Why do the men harness Dave with the team, although he is clearly dying?** Dave is a quiet dog who has lived for the sole purpose of working on the trail and working well. Though he has become too sick to do his job, he persists in taking his place with the team. The men admire Dave and allow him to continue working for the sake of his honor.

Make A Prediction:

Buck has conquered his enemy, Spitz, and has overcome many difficulties to take over the leadership of the dog team. Predict Buck's next challenge.

Guided Discussion:

Discuss some of the key questions in Section II. In addition, feel free to include in your discussion questions that are not in the Discussion Guide.

Vocabulary Prediction Check-up

Return to the vocabulary prediction chart, and use it to check the predictions students made prior to reading this section of the reading selection. Remind students that, even if their predictions did not prove true, the value was in making them.

 Selection Review

1. **Why does Francois and Perrault's dog sled team begin doing a poor job?** When Buck openly and continually challenges Spitz's leadership of the dog sled team, the team becomes much less effective in its work. The dogs quarrel among themselves and do not work together.

2. **How has Buck shown that he has conquered the law of the club and the fang?** When Buck cunningly and savagely defeats Spitz, he shows he has conquered the law of the fang. When Buck avoids Francois and Perrault's club, while getting them to obey his wishes, he shows he has conquered the law of the club.

3. **How do you know that Buck is pleased with his new home and the changes that have come over him in the Northland?** Buck's dreams of his ancestors reveal that he is pleased with his new home in the Northland. These overwhelming dreams of prehistoric existence reflect the change in Buck's inner state. He is no longer the civilized dog of the Southland, but is becoming more and more like his uncivilized ancestors.

4. **Give at least two examples of the struggle for survival in chapters 3 and 4.** The huskies that raid the camp are starving. They viciously attack the dogs in camp in order to find food for their survival. Both the men and the dogs show great strength and determination in their journey on the dangerous trail. Whenever a man or dog slips through the ice into the

water, the group must stop and build a fire to dry out. Otherwise, they would die. The greatest fight for survival comes when Buck and Spitz fight to the death in the climax of this chapter. In chapter 4, Dave's courageous will to live and work is shown, but his struggle ends in death.

5. **How has Buck shown himself to be superior to Spitz in chapters 3 and 4?** Buck shows his superiority to Spitz in the their struggle to the death. Buck uses his cunning mind to defeat Spitz. He also shows his superiority as the leader of the dogsled team. Buck is able to get the dogs to perform their work much better than even Spitz could.

 Literature-Related Writing

1. An **epitaph** is a saying written on a tomb or gravestone in memory of the person buried there. Write epitaphs for both Spitz's and Dave's tombstones. Make the epitaphs reflect their characters and lives.

2. Pretend that the Canadian government needs more dispatchers to perform work similar to that of Francois and Perrault. Write a **classified advertisement** for a Canadian newspaper describing the job. Describe the job's challenges and benefits.

3. Buck's Northland environment is governed by the law of the club and the fang. He has learned how to survive in the context of these laws. Give a name to the "law" under which you must live. Describe this **law** and explain how you have learned to live with it.

Extension Activities

1. Do research on dog sledding. How does today's dog sledding compare and contrast to the dog sledding described in *The Call of the Wild*? Is dog sledding still used for work or only for sport? Tell your classmates what you learn from your research.

2. Draw a scene from one of Buck's dreams.

3. Design a book cover for *The Call of the Wild* that reflects its survival theme.

4. Create symbols to represent the law of the fang and the law of the club.

Literature Test

1. **How does the conflict between Buck and Spitz affect the dog sled team?** When Buck openly and continually challenges Spitz's leadership of the dog sled team, the team becomes much less effective in its work. The dogs quarrel among themselves and do not work together.

2. **What law governs the Northland? How has Buck shown that he has conquered this law?** The Northland is ruled by the law of the club and fang. When Buck cunningly and savagely defeats Spitz, he shows he has conquered the law of the fang. When Buck avoids Francois and Perrault's club, while getting them to obey his wishes, he shows he has conquered the law of the club.

3. **What does Buck dream about when he sits by the warm fire at night? What do these dreams tell you about Buck?** Buck dreams of his home in the Santa Clara Valley, but he is not homesick and has no desire to return to his former way of life. Much stronger are the visions of his ancestors. These overwhelming dreams of prehistoric existence reflect the change

in Buck's inner state. He is no longer the civilized dog of the Southland, but is becoming more and more like his uncivilized ancestors.

4. **What enables Buck to kill the experienced fighter, Spitz?**
When Spitz and Buck fight by instinct, Spitz dominates the fight. Buck changes his strategy. He uses his mind to overcome Spitz. He devises a clever trick to cripple and kill Spitz.

Discussion Guide #3

Chapters 5 and 6

Vocabulary List A

*feigned (p. 66)
fatigue (n., p. 66)
*taut (p. 67)
salient (p. 68)
callowness (p. 68)
unutterable (p. 68)
slovenly (p. 68)
repugnance (p. 70)

clannish (p. 71)
superfluous (p. 73)
*discarded (adj., p. 73)
averred (p. 73)
famine (p. 77)
voracious (p. 77)
copious (p. 80)

prerogative (p. 80)
perambulating (p. 82)
wayfarers (p. 84)
innocuously (p. 84)
terse (p. 84)
impending (p. 86)
*inarticulate (p. 86)
*chaotic (p. 87)

Special Glossary

mongrels - mixed-breeds

fissures - long, deep cracks

Glossary of Starred Words

feigned - pretended; faked

taut - tightly stretched, as a rope

discarded - thrown away

inarticulate - without understandable words

chaotic - disorderly; disorganized

Sample Meaningful Sentences for Starred Words

1. The boy **feigned** an illness so he could stay home from school, but his mother began to suspect that he was not really sick because he seemed full of energy.

2. When the rope Tom had tied between the trees began to droop, he pulled it **taut** and tied it again to make it straight and tight.

3. Joey searched the trash bag hoping to find something useful in it, but the **discarded** toys were worn or broken.

4. The old, sickly man spoke in an **inarticulate** whisper, so no one was sure what he wanted.

5. Mrs. Wilson's students usually pay attention and work hard, but things became **chaotic** when a squirrel entered the room and students got out of their seats and began talking excitedly.

 The Writer's Craft

Foreshadowing and *Alliteration*

Foreshadowing occurs in a story when the author gives clues about events yet to come. As you read the beginning of chapter 5, watch for these kinds of hints. Make a prediction about what will happen later in the chapter.

Alliteration is the repetition of an initial consonant sound, as in "**r**ough and **r**eady" and "**sl**owing **sl**ipping." Alliteration is often used in poetry. Alliteration produces a pleasing sound, and phrases containing alliteration are especially enjoyable when read out loud. The following chapter contains many examples of alliteration. See if you can find them, and say the phrases out loud.

DISCUSSION QUESTIONS AND ACTIVITIES

Section I. Read chapter 5 (pages 66-88). Discuss answers to the following questions with a classmate, then write your answers independently.

1. **What hints at the beginning of the chapter *foreshadow* that Buck's new journey will be a tragic one?** Many statements at the beginning of chapter 5 hint that things will not go well on Buck's journey. It is clear that Buck's new owners, Hal, Charles, and Mercedes are "out of place" in the Northland. They know almost nothing about the dangers and challenges that lie ahead on the trip or how to prepare for them. It is also clear that Buck and the other dogs they have bought are too tired to make the journey. Buck is nervous when he discovers what his new owners are like because he knows that he cannot trust them. All of these things strongly hint that the trip will not be a successful one.

2. **Describe Buck's new owners, Hal, Charles, and Mercedes. How do they contrast with Buck's former owners in the Northland?** Hal, Charles, and Mercedes are from the States, the Southland, and are ill-equipped for the Northland. They are ignorant of the Northland's ways and foolishly expect to transport their comforts and possessions from the South to their new home in the North. They are ignorant about survival and refuse to learn. They reject the advice of the more experienced travelers. They are lazy, disorderly, and know little about dogs. In contrast, Buck's former owners have known how to handle the dogs and have treated them fairly. The former owners were hard, patient workers, but this new trio of owners "not only [do] not know how to work the dogs, they [do] not know how to work themselves."

3. **Several new dogs from the Southland are added to Buck's team. They become spirit-broken because they cannot handle their ill-treatment or harsh new environment. Buck, however, was able to rise above similar circumstances when he first arrived in the Northland and become an outstanding contributor to his dog team. What qualities make Buck different from these other dogs? Explain your answer.**

Students' answers will vary. Accept supported answers. Possible answers follow. 1) Buck considered everything that happened to him and learned ways to respond and survive. He developed cunning and used his mind to develop strategies of survival. Instead of being defeated by the law of the club and the fang, he became wise in the way of the law and learned to rise above it. 2) Unlike the newcomers, Buck never allowed his spirit to be broken. Even when Hal beat him almost to the point of death, Buck refused to go with the dog sled team. Buck is sure the travelers are doomed and refuses to go with them. Buck's determination and boldness of spirit save his life while all others in the team perish. 3) Buck learns to enjoy the savage way of life. He becomes increasingly primitive. He enjoys the life of his ancestors so completely, he does not even miss his former home in the Southland.

4. **How does the spring weather contrast with what is happening among the dogs and their owners?** It is springtime in the Northland. There is an awakening in the cold, frozen land now "fraught with the joy of living." Things dead or silent have come to life, and there is a flurry of activity. In contrast, the dogs are starving, spiritless, and near death. Charles, Hal, and Mercedes are exhausted and argue among themselves continuously. They are described as "wayfarers to death."

5. **How does Buck show he is wiser and more fit for survival than Charles, Hal, and Mercedes?** Charles, Hal, and Mercedes refuse to heed the warnings given to them about the melting ice and fall through the ice and are killed along with their dog sled team. But Buck, who had sensed their impending doom, refused to leave camp to go with them. He remains behind in John Thornton's camp while the rest of the travelers perish.

Make A
Prediction:

Will Buck stay with John Thornton? What will his life be like now?

Guided Discussion:

Discuss some of the key questions in Section I. In addition, feel free to include in your discussion questions that are not in the Discussion Guide, such as: *What examples of **alliteration** did you find?* The chapter's title contains alliteration: *The **T**oil of the **T**race and **T**rail.* Pages 82 and 83 contain many examples of alliteration including the following: ***d**ull and **d**istant, **b**ags of **b**ones, **f**luttered **f**aintly, **f**luttered **f**eebly, **d**ead **d**ogs, **g**arbs of **g**reen,* and ***cr**eeping, **cr**awling things.*

 Vocabulary Prediction Check-up

Return to the vocabulary prediction chart, and use it to check the predictions students made prior to reading this section of the reading selection. Remind students that, even if their predictions did not prove true, the value was in making them.

Vocabulary List B

demonstrative (p. 90)	peremptorily (p. 94)	repose (n., p. 104)
convalescence (p. 90)	*uncanny (p. 96)	*vigor (p. 104)
*pompous (p. 90)	extremity (p. 100)	conjuration (p. 105)
caress (n., p. 91)	*exploit (n., p. 101)	*incoherent (p. 107)
transient (p. 92)	contagion (p. 104)	babel (p. 107)
wiliness (p. 93)	virility (p. 104)	indiscreet (p. 108)

Special Glossary

tenderfoot - a newcomer who is not used to the hardship associated with the work or the area

totem pole - a pole created by some northwest coastal Indian tribes; it contained carvings of animals and symbols that told memorable stories about tribal people and events.

Glossary of Starred Words

pompous - puffed up; proud; self-important

uncanny - remarkable; extraordinary; hard to explain

exploit - a daring deed or act; an accomplishment

vigor - energy; strength (spelled "vigour" in *The Call of the Wild*)

incoherent - rambling in thought or speech; mixed-up; confused

Sample Meaningful Sentences for Starred Words

1. The **pompous** child expected family members to treat her like a princess, and she pouted whenever she didn't get her way.

2. The detective said the robbery was **uncanny** because there were no signs of a break-in, and she has no clue as to how the robbery was carried out.

3. The firefighter showed great bravery when he rescued the child from the burning building, and he received a special award for his **exploit**.

4. Anna's grandmother, who had been very active, lost her **vigor** as she grew older and could no longer walk without help.

5. When the emergency workers arrived at the scene of the accident, the sobbing woman was **incoherent** and could not explain what had happened to her.

DISCUSSION QUESTIONS AND ACTIVITIES

Section II. Read chapter 6 (pages 89-108). Discuss answers to the following questions with a classmate, then write your answers independently.

1. **What does Buck experience for the first time in John Thornton's camp?** In John Thornton's camp "genuine passionate love was Buck's for the first time." Buck has had partnerships, business relationships, and even friendships with his former owners. However, John Thornton is a perfect master and treats Buck like a son. This is a new experience for Buck, and he loves and adores Thornton.

2. **How has Buck become famous throughout Alaska?** Buck performs amazing feats out of his devotion to his master, John Thornton. Buck attacks and kills a man who is trying to harm Thornton. He saves Thornton from drowning in a raging river. He defies all odds by pulling a thousand pound load for one hundred yards on a bet that Thornton initiated.

3. **What is the call that Buck begins to hear? How does Buck's relationship with John Thornton affect how he responds to the call?** Buck begins to hear a mysterious call beckoning him deep into the forest. The call is urging Buck to leave what little attachment he has to the civilized world to become completely wild. The call is very appealing to Buck, but his love for John Thornton prevents him from heeding it. Thornton is Buck's only remaining attachment to civilization.

Prediction:

Will Buck eventually listen to "the call of the wild," or will he remain attached to the civilized world? Predict the story's ending.

Guided Discussion:

Discuss some of the key questions in Section II. In addition, feel free to include in your discussion questions that are not in the Discussion Guide.

 Vocabulary Prediction Check-up

Return to the vocabulary prediction chart, and use it to check the predictions students made prior to reading this section of the reading selection. Remind students that, even if their predictions did not prove true, the value was in making them.

 Selection Review

1. **What early hints suggest that Hal, Charles, and Mercedes will not survive in the Northland?** Hal, Charles, and Mercedes are from the States, the Southland, and are not prepared for life in the Northland. They are ignorant of the Northland's ways and foolishly expect to travel with a large number of possessions. They are ignorant about survival and refuse to learn from the advice of more experienced travelers. The three travelers are lazy, disorderly, and know little about dogs. Hal, Charles, and Mercedes are "out of place" in the Northland, and it is clear that they will not survive.

2. **How is Buck able to avoid the fatal trip that leads to Charles, Hal, and Mercedes' death?** When the team leaves John Thornton's camp, Buck senses that something bad is going to happen, and refuses to leave camp with them. John Thornton rescues Buck from Hal's terrible beating, and the team leaves without Buck. Not long after the team leaves camp, they break through thin ice and die.

3. **Explain Buck's rise to fame.** Buck performs amazing feats out of his devotion to his master, John Thornton. Buck attacks and kills a man who is trying to harm Thornton. He saves Thornton from drowning in a raging river. He goes against all odds by pulling a thousand pound load for one hundred yards on a bet that Thornton started.

4. **What is calling Buck deep in the forest? Why is Buck not willing to follow the call?** Buck begins to hear a mysterious call deep in the forest. The call is urging Buck to leave what little attachment he has to the civilized world to become completely wild. The call is very appealing to Buck, but his love for John Thornton prevents him from listening to it. Thornton is his only remaining attachment to civilization.

 Literature-Related Writing

1. Write a **news article** for an Alaskan newspaper that features the famous dog Buck.

2. Write a **ballad**, a poem or song that tells a story, about Hal, Charles, and Mercedes' experience in the Northland.

3. Write a **letter** of advice from Buck to a group of dogs that have just arrived in the Northland on how to cope in their new environment.

4. Write a **skit** about Hal, Charles, and Mercedes' trip. Perform it for your classmates.

 Extension Activities

1. Learn more about totem poles. Create a small totem pole of symbols that represent memorable events in your own life.

2. Draw a picture of springtime in the Northland as it is described in chapter 5.

3. Research Charles Darwin's concept of the "survival of the fittest." Find out how this concept is used in *The Call of the Wild.* Share what you learn with your classmates.

Literature Test

1. **If Buck could speak, what would he have told Hal, Charles, and Mercedes about how to survive in the Northland?** Students' answers will vary. Accept reasonable answers. Possible answers include: Observe closely to learn about the dangers of life in the Northland. Don't take these dangers lightly, and be prepared to face them. Follow the advice of people who have lived and traveled successfully in the Northland. Treat your dog team kindly and protect their health because your lives depend on them. Be willing to give up the comforts of the Southland.

2. **In what way are Hal, Charles, and Mercedes responsible for their own deaths?** In a certain sense, Hal, Charles, and Mercedes are responsible for their own deaths. They are not prepared to live in the Northland. They do not understand how dangerous it is and how different it is from the Southland. They do not listen to the advice of other people who know more about the dangers of traveling in the Northland. Even when their dogs are dying, Hal, Charles, and Mercedes refuse to turn back or seek help. They die as a result of their pride and foolishness.

3. **Explain how Buck avoids being killed along with the rest of his team.** When the team leaves John Thornton's camp, Buck senses an impending doom, and refuses to leave camp with them. John Thornton rescues Buck from a brutal beating, and the team leaves without Buck. Not long after the team leaves camp, they break through thin ice and perish.

4. **What is the motivation behind Buck's incredible accomplishments that bring him fame?** Buck is motivated out of his passionate love and complete devotion to his master, John Thornton.

5. **What is the "call of the wild"? Why isn't Buck responding to it?** The call of the wild is a mysterious call beckoning to Buck from deep in the forest. The call is urging Buck to leave what little attachment he has to the civilized world to become completely wild. The call is very appealing to Buck, but his love for John Thornton prevents him from responding to it. Thornton is Buck's only remaining attachment to civilization.

Discussion Guide #4

Chapter 7

Teachers' Note: There is only one section to this Discussion Guide.

Vocabulary List

melancholy (adj., p. 111)	*coy (p. 116)	palpitant (p. 124)
obliterated (p. 111)	belie (p. 116)	certitude (p. 125)
salient (p. 112)	lope (n., p. 118)	*calamity (p. 125)
subdued (p. 114)	infinitesimal (p. 120)	*stealthily (p. 125)
truce (p. 115)	wantonness (p. 121)	excrescence (p. 126)
commingled (p. 115)	*formidable (p. 121)	*usurp (p. 126)
pertinacity (p. 116)	paroxysms (p. 122)	sluice (adj., p. 128)
	ambuscade (p. 122)	discomfited (p. 131)

Glossary of Starred Words

coy - shy; unassuming; timid

formidable - powerful; mighty

calamity - disaster; tragedy

stealthily - sneakily; slyly; secretly

usurp - to take over; to take power

Sample Meaningful Sentences for Starred Words

1. The **coy** puppy seemed uneasy around people, and spent most of its time hiding under the table.

2. The players knew that their next opponent was a **formidable** one, and that they would have to play their best in order to have any chance of winning.

3. The hurricane brought great destruction to the seaside town, and the town's mayor appeared on the news to talk about the **calamity**.

4. The boy had been **stealthily** taking the forbidden cookies from the cookie container, and his mother did not realize what he was doing until they were almost gone.

5. Tim had been the recognized playground leader at recess time, but a new boy named Eddie arrived and began to **usurp** Tim's position by convincing kids to follow him instead.

 The Writer's Craft

Symbolism

A **symbol** is a real thing used to represent an idea. Examples of symbols include our nation's use of the bald eagle to represent American freedom, a dove used to represent peace, and the seasons spring and winter to represent youth and old age. Symbolism in literature can also be present when a word is used to represent an idea that goes beyond the meaning of the word. For example, the color yellow might be used to represent cowardice in a novel, or the color black might be used to represent death.

continued...

Writers often use or create symbols, and the alert reader will watch for them as he or she reads. The repeated use of an object, idea, action, etc., is a hint that it is being used symbolically. Often the reader may have the sense that something written in the story could have a meaning beyond its literal meaning. When the reader senses this, he or she should look for clues in the story that support that possibility.

In *The Call of the Wild*, author Jack London has created several symbols to represent the primitive life. These have been used over and over throughout the novel and should not be too difficult to identify. Many of these symbols appear in the story's final chapter. Watch for them as you read.

DISCUSSION QUESTIONS AND ACTIVITIES

Read chapter 7 (pages 109-134). Discuss answers to the following questions with a classmate, then write your answers independently.

1. **What symbols used in chapter 7 are also used throughout the novel as representations of the primitive life?** The forest, the pre-historic man, the howl of the wolf, and the wolf itself are all used repeatedly in *The Call of the Wild* as symbols of the primitive life.

2. **How are Buck's hunting strategies and skills emphasized in this chapter? What is the author trying to say about Buck by emphasizing these things?** This chapter emphasizes Buck's changing attitude toward hunting. Even though he does not need to hunt for his food, he begins to do so because "he prefer[s] to eat what he kill[s] himself." The smaller animals he eats become too easy for him to catch and kill, however, so he begins looking for a more powerful prey. He chooses a large moose bull and shows great patience, cunning, and skill to eventually kill it. Author Jack London emphasizes Buck's hunting to point out how completely he has adapted to the wild. Buck is not only more than capable of feeding himself, but he takes great enjoyment in the challenge of catching large prey.

3. **How does the moose herd respond to Buck's pursuit of their leader? How does their response relate to the message of survival in this story?** The moose herd's abandonment of the once strong and dominant bull in order to protect their own interests and survival depicts the harsh reality of survival in the wild. Initially when Buck attempts an attack on the old bull, the young bulls protect him, but Buck's persistence in harassing the bull slows down the herd. The herd finally leaves the old bull behind because, after all, "the life of only one member was demanded... and in the end they were content to pay the toll."

4. **To a certain degree, John Thornton and Buck are similar characters and have led similar lives. List these similarities.** Buck and John Thornton are the novel's noblest characters. Thornton and Buck are alike in that they are both capable and adaptable. They both have a strong sense of fairness. Both fare well in civilized and uncivilized environments, yet both have a great love for the wilderness. Both have had to face tremendous struggles for survival against nature and against men.

5. **Why does Buck kill the Yeehat Indians? Why does he take great pride in his action?** Buck kills the Yeehat Indians because they killed John Thornton. Buck is proud because "he has killed man, the noblest game of all." Buck had already shown his dominance over beast, and now he has overcome man, whom he will never fear again.

Guided Discussion:

Discuss some of the key questions in the section. In addition, feel free to include in your discussion questions that are not in the Discussion Guide.

Vocabulary Prediction Check-up

Return to the vocabulary prediction chart, and use it to check the predictions students made prior to reading this section of the reading selection. Remind students that, even if their predictions did not prove true, the value was in making them.

 Selection Review

1. **Why does the call of the wild become stronger in Buck's life as the end of the novel nears?** Throughout the novel, Buck has become increasingly adapted to the harsh, uncivilized life in the Northland. His behavior in chapter 7 shows that he is ready to live in the wild. The call becomes so strong that Buck will no longer refuse it.

2. **What does the moose herd's behavior towards the old bull teach about survival?** The moose herd's willingness to leave its leader in order to protect its own interests and survival shows the harshness of survival in the wild. When Buck first attempts to attack the old bull, the young bulls protect him. But Buck's determination in harassing the bull slows down the herd. The herd finally leaves the old bull behind because, after all, "the life of only one member was demanded... and in the end they were content to pay the toll."

3. **Why does Buck prove to be more fit for survival than John Thornton?** John Thornton is wise, capable, and adaptable, and is the noblest human character in *The Call of the Wild*. But Buck's animal instincts and his return to his primitive state have proven him more adapted for survival than Thornton.

4. **Why does Buck become a Yeehat Indian legend?** Buck's murder of Yeehat Indians becomes well-known, and he is greatly feared. He is known as the Ghost Dog who is brave and strong and more cunning than man.

Literature-Related Writing

1. Write your own Indian **legend** about Buck.

2. Create your own **symbol** of the wild. Write a descriptive paragraph using the symbol.

3. Write a **poem** that reflects Jack London's perspective on survival and the importance of primitive instincts.

 Extension Activities

1. Depict the "call of the wild" in a drawing or painting.

2. Research wolves. Find out how true wolf behavior compares and contrasts with the wolf behavior described in this novel. Share what you learn with your classmates.

3. One reason that *The Call of the Wild* has been a popular book is because of its setting in the beautiful Alaskan wilderness. Jack London lived there and was able to bring its scenes alive to the reader. Choose an unusual and appealing setting for a novel. Describe the setting and explain why you believe it would be appealing to readers.

Literature Test

1. **Why does Buck choose to hunt the moose bull? How is this a change from the past?** The smaller animals that Buck hunts and eats have become too easy for him to catch and kill, so he begins looking for a more powerful prey. He chooses a large moose bull. This is a change from the past because Buck has not previously hunted simply for the pleasure of it. He does not hunt only to eat, but for the thrill of the challenge.

2. **Tell how Buck and John Thornton are alike.** Buck and John Thornton are the novel's noblest characters. Thornton and Buck are alike in that they are both capable and adaptable. They both have a strong sense of fairness. Both fare well in civilized and uncivilized environments, yet both have a great love for the wilderness. Both have had to face tremendous struggles for survival against nature and against men.

3. **Why is Buck's murder of Yeehat Indians his greatest victory?**
Buck's murder of several Yeehat Indians is his greatest victory because man is "the noblest game of all." Buck has already shown his dominance over animals, and now he has overcome man, whom he will never fear again.

4. **Although Buck and John Thornton are similar in many ways, there are also differences between them. Which one is more fit for survival? How do we know? What message do you think author Jack London is expressing by ending the novel this way?** Buck is clearly portrayed as being more fit for survival than John Thornton. This is evident from the fact that Thornton falls prey to the Yeehat Indians and is killed, but Buck triumphs over the Yeehat and kills them. Students' answers may vary as to what London's message is; accept reasonable answers supported with thoughtful discussion. One possible answer is that London is showing the superiority of those who live closest to nature. The Yeehat, who are more "primitive" and closer to the wild than Thornton, are able to kill him. Buck, however, despite his "civilized" origins, has developed his physical and mental toughness through living in the wild to the point that he is victorious over the Yeehat and is able to kill them. This ensures his own survival and avenges the death of Thornton.

Selection Review #1

The Call of the Wild

Chapters 1-2

1. **Why does Buck come to the Northland? Why are Buck's new circumstances so shocking to him?** A man working for Buck's owner needs money, so he sells Buck without the owner's knowledge. Buck is sold to men in the Northland, the cold harsh region north of the continental United States. There is a gold rush in the Northland. The men who search for gold need strong, long-haired dogs to pull their sleds through the frozen wilderness. Buck has been used to a pleasant, easy life in the Santa Clara Valley. After he is sold he is shocked by the harsh, cruel treatment he receives.

2. **Explain the statement, "[Buck] had been suddenly jerked from the heart of civilization and flung into the heart of things primordial." Use examples from the novel to support your answer.** Author Jack London associates the pleasant, orderly, moral lifestyle of the Southland with civilization. He associates the harsh struggle and the unfair, immoral nature of the Northland with primitive life. This statement means that Buck has been taken away from a civilized life and placed in a primitive one.

3. **What is the "law of the club and fang," and how does Buck learn it?** The law of the club and the fang is the rule of power and physical force. Buck learns the law of the club from the red-sweatered man in chapter 1, who beats Buck into obedience. Buck learns the law of the fang from the terrible attack on Curly.

4. **How does Buck begin to change in order to survive in his new surroundings?** In order to survive, Buck has to forget the way he interacted with other animals and people in the Southland. Buck begins to depend on his instincts to survive. He rejects the morality of the Southland, which is "a handicap in the ruthless struggle for existence." He learns to steal when he is hungry. Physically, he also adapts. He becomes hardened toward ordinary pain, learns to eat whatever is available, and develops sharper senses.

5. **Describe Buck's relationship with Spitz, the leader of the dog team. Make a prediction about their relationship, giving reasons to support your prediction.** Spitz, the dog team leader, is described as a smart, skilled sled team leader. However, he has a hardened, cruel nature, which angers Buck. Spitz laughs when Curly is killed by a group of other dogs. When Buck sees this, he begins to hate Spitz "with a bitter and deathless hatred." This description of Buck's feelings towards Spitz is so strong, it hints at a future conflict between the two dogs. Predictions about the nature of this conflict will vary. Be sure you present reasons that support your predictions.

Selection Review #2

The Call of the Wild

Chapters 3-4

1. **Why does Francois and Perrault's dog sled team begin doing a poor job?** When Buck openly and continually challenges Spitz's leadership of the dog sled team, the team becomes much less effective in its work. The dogs quarrel among themselves and do not work together.

2. **How has Buck shown that he has conquered the law of the club and the fang?** When Buck cunningly and savagely defeats Spitz, he shows he has conquered the law of the fang. When Buck avoids Francois and Perrault's club, while getting them to obey his wishes, he shows he has conquered the law of the club.

3. **How do you know that Buck is pleased with his new home and the changes that have come over him in the Northland?** Buck's dreams of his ancestors reveal that he is pleased with his new home in the Northland. These overwhelming dreams of prehistoric existence reflect the change in Buck's inner state. He is no longer the civilized dog of the Southland, but is becoming more and more like his uncivilized ancestors.

4. **Give at least two examples of the struggle for survival in chapters 3 and 4.** The huskies that raid the camp are starving. They viciously attack the dogs in camp in order to find food for their survival. Both the men and the dogs show great strength and determination in their journey on the dangerous trail. Whenever a man or dog slips through the ice into the water, the group must stop and build a fire to dry out. Otherwise, they would die. The greatest fight for survival comes when Buck and Spitz fight to the death in the climax of this chapter. In chapter 4, Dave's courageous will to live and work is shown, but his struggle ends in death.

5. **How has Buck shown himself to be superior to Spitz in chapters 3 and 4?** Buck shows his superiority to Spitz in the their struggle to the death. Buck uses his cunning mind to defeat Spitz. He also shows his superiority as the leader of the dogsled team. Buck is able to get the dogs to perform their work much better than even Spitz could.

Selection Review #3

The Call of the Wild

Chapters 5-6

1. **What early hints suggest that Hal, Charles, and Mercedes will not survive in the Northland?** Hal, Charles, and Mercedes are from the States, the Southland, and are not prepared for life in the Northland. They are ignorant of the Northland's ways and foolishly expect to travel with a large number of possessions. They are ignorant about survival and refuse to learn from the advice of more experienced travelers. The three travelers are lazy, disorderly, and know little about dogs. Hal, Charles, and Mercedes are "out of place" in the Northland, and it is clear that they will not survive.

2. **How is Buck able to avoid the fatal trip that leads to Charles, Hal, and Mercedes' death?** When the team leaves John Thornton's camp, Buck senses that something bad is going to happen, and refuses to leave camp with them. John Thornton rescues Buck from Hal's terrible beating, and the team leaves without Buck. Not long after the team leaves camp, they break through thin ice and die.

3. **Explain Buck's rise to fame.** Buck performs amazing feats out of his devotion to his master, John Thornton. Buck attacks and kills a man who is trying to harm Thornton. He saves Thornton from drowning in a raging river. He goes against all odds by pulling a thousand pound load for one hundred yards on a bet that Thornton started.

4. **What is calling Buck deep in the forest? Why is Buck not willing to follow the call?** Buck begins to hear a mysterious call deep in the forest. The call is urging Buck to leave what little attachment he has to the civilized world to become completely wild. The call is very appealing to Buck, but his love for John Thornton prevents him from listening to it. Thornton is his only remaining attachment to civilization.

Selection Review #4

The Call of the Wild

Chapter 7

1. **Why does the call of the wild become stronger in Buck's life as the end of the novel nears?** Throughout the novel, Buck has become increasingly adapted to the harsh, uncivilized life in the Northland. His behavior in chapter 7 shows that he is ready to live in the wild. The call becomes so strong that Buck will no longer refuse it.

2. **What does the moose herd's behavior towards the old bull teach about survival?** The moose herd's willingness to leave its leader in order to protect its own interests and survival shows the harshness of survival in the wild. When Buck first attempts to attack the old bull, the young bulls protect him. But Buck's determination in harassing the bull slows down the herd. The herd finally leaves the old bull behind because, after all, "the life of only one member was demanded... and in the end they were content to pay the toll."

3. **Why does Buck prove to be more fit for survival than John Thornton?** John Thornton is wise, capable, and adaptable, and is the noblest human character in *The Call of the Wild*. But Buck's animal instincts and his return to his primitive state have proven him more adapted for survival than Thornton.

4. **Why does Buck become a Yeehat Indian legend?** Buck's murder of Yeehat Indians becomes well-known, and he is greatly feared. He is known as the Ghost Dog who is brave and strong and more cunning than man.

Name: _____

Literature Test #1

The Call of the Wild

Chapters 1-2

1. What law rules the Northland? Describe this law.

_____

_____

_____

_____

_____

_____

_____

2. How is life in the Southland different from life in the Northland?

_____

_____

_____

_____

_____

_____

_____

continued...

3. What changes in Buck show that he is "fit to survive" in the Northland?

_____

_____

_____

_____

_____

_____

_____

4. What does author Jack London mean when he describes the Northland as being "primordial"?

_____

_____

_____

_____

_____

_____

_____

5. How do you think Buck's view of men and animals has changed as a result of his experiences in the Northland? Explain your answer.

_____

_____

_____

_____

_____

_____

_____

Name:

Literature Test #2

The Call of the Wild

Chapters 3-4

1. How does the conflict between Buck and Spitz affect the dog sled team?

_____

_____

_____

_____

_____

_____

2. What law governs the Northland? How has Buck shown that he has conquered this law?

_____

_____

_____

_____

_____

_____

_____

continued...

3. What does Buck dream about when he sits by the warm fire at night? What do these dreams tell you about Buck?

_____

_____

_____

_____

_____

_____

_____

4. What enables Buck to kill the experienced fighter, Spitz?

_____

_____

_____

_____

_____

_____

_____

Name: _____

Literature Test #3

The Call of the Wild

Chapters 5–6

1. If Buck could speak, what would he have told Hal, Charles, and Mercedes about how to survive in the Northland?

_____

_____

_____

_____

_____

_____

2. In what way are Hal, Charles, and Mercedes responsible for their own deaths?

_____

_____

_____

_____

_____

_____

continued...

3. Explain how Buck avoids being killed along with the rest of his team.

_____

_____

_____

_____

_____

_____

_____

4. What is the motivation behind Buck's incredible accomplishments that bring him fame?

_____

_____

_____

_____

_____

_____

_____

5. What is the "call of the wild"? Why isn't Buck responding to it?

_____

_____

_____

_____

_____

_____

_____

Name:

Literature Test #4

The Call of the Wild

Chapter 7

1. Why does Buck choose to hunt the moose bull? How is this a change from the past?

_____

_____

_____

_____

_____

_____

_____

2. Tell how Buck and John Thornton are alike.

_____

_____

_____

_____

_____

_____

_____

continued...

3. Why is Buck's murder of Yeehat Indians his greatest victory?

_____

_____

_____

_____

_____

_____

4. Although Buck and John Thornton are similar in many ways, there are also differences between them. Which one is more fit for survival? How do we know? What message do you think author Jack London is expressing by ending the novel this way?

_____

_____

_____

_____

_____

_____

Name:

Vocabulary Test #1

The Call of the Wild

Chapters 1-2

WRITE SENTENCES FOR THE FOLLOWING WORDS:

egotistical   futilely   intolerable

impending   taunted   perpetual

despise   malignant   callous

conspicuous

_____

_____

_____

_____

_____

_____

_____

_____

_____

_____

_____

_____

_____

Name: _____

Vocabulary Test #2

The Call of the Wild

Chapters 3-4

WRITE SENTENCES FOR THE FOLLOWING WORDS:

dominant	daunted	defied
shirked	rampant	coveted
sheepishly	monotonous	potent

_____

_____

_____

_____

_____

_____

_____

_____

_____

_____

_____

_____

_____

Name: _____

Vocabulary Test #3

The Call of the Wild

Chapters 5-6

WRITE SENTENCES FOR THE FOLLOWING WORDS:

feigned	taut	discarded
inarticulate	chaotic	pompous
uncanny	exploit	vigor
	incoherent	

_____

_____

_____

_____

_____

_____

_____

_____

_____

_____

_____

_____

Name: _____

Vocabulary Test #4

The Call of the Wild

Chapter 7

WRITE SENTENCES FOR THE FOLLOWING WORDS:

coy   formidable   calamity

stealthily   usurp

_____

_____

_____

_____

_____

_____

_____

_____

_____

_____

_____

_____

_____

_____

Student Team Literature Discussion Guides are available for the following titles:

Non-fiction

The Acorn People

Anne Frank: The Diary of a Young Girl

Barack Obama: President for a New Era

Barack Obama: United States President

The Double Life of Pocahontas

First They Killed My Father

Freedom Train

Freedom's Children

Leon's Story

One More River to Cross: the Stories of Twelve Black Americans

Warriors Don't Cry

We Beat the Street

What's the Big Idea, Ben Franklin?

Short Stories, Poetry, and Mythology

Beowulf: A New Telling

The Dark-Thirty: Southern Tales of the Supernatural

A Dime a Dozen

The Dream Keeper and Other Poems

ego-tripping and other poems for young people

Keeping the Night Watch

The Library Card

Locomotion

Make Lemonade

The Odyssey, retold by Robin Lister

Novels

The Big Wave

Bridge to Terabithia

Bud, Not Buddy

The Bully

Call It Courage

The Call of the Wild

The Cay

Crash

Curse of a Winter Moon

Darnell Rock Reporting

A Day No Pigs Would Die

Eddie's Ordeal

Esperanza Rising

Fast Sam, Cool Clyde, and Stuff

Freak the Mighty

The Giver

Hatchet

The Hobbit

Holes

In the Night, on Lanvale Street

Jacob Have I Loved

Johnny Tremain

Journey

Justin and the Best Biscuits in the World

M. C. Higgins the Great

Maniac Magee

The Midwife's Apprentice

Monster

The Mystery of Apartment A-13

Ninjas, Piranhas, and Galileo

Nothing But the Truth

Number the Stars

The Outsiders

The Pinballs

Roll of Thunder, Hear My Cry

Sing Down the Moon

The Skin I'm In

To Kill a Mockingbird

Touching Spirit Bear

Tuck Everlasting

The Watsons Go to Birmingham—1963

The Westing Game

The Whipping Boy

Wringer

A Wrinkle in Time

Yolonda's Genius

For a catalog and ordering information, call 410-516-4339
For information on Student Team Literature professional development,
call Maria Waltemeyer (410-516-2247)
or visit the Talent Development Secondary website at
www.talentdevelopmentsecondary.com